CW00345051

Joy

'I have had the JOY of reading this book in advance and I am excited. I also know most of the authors personally and that they have or had a strong walk with God. Their challenging messages have been a huge help and blessing in my life.'
George Verwer, founder of Operation Mobilisation, author and speaker

'A rich feast! Ranging through a variety of scriptures, this book reminds us that joy is not an optional extra but the natural overflow of a life centred on Jesus. We often have to fight for joy – it is not a matter of temperament, circumstances or passing feelings. We can still have joy in Jesus, even when there are tears in our eyes. I enthusiastically commend this book.'
Edrie Mallard, mentor whose joy, despite having multiple sclerosis, is legendary

30-DAY DEVOTIONAL

Joy

Edited by Elizabeth McQuoid

Keswick
Resources

FOOD
FOR THE
JOURNEY

INTER-VARSITY PRESS
36 Causton Street, London SW1P 4ST, England
Email: ivp@ivpbooks.com
Website: www.ivpbooks.com

© Keswick Ministries, 2020

Elizabeth McQuoid has asserted her right under the Copyright, Designs and Patents Act 1988 to be identified as Author of this work.

All rights reserved. No part of this publication may be reproduced, stored in a retrieval system, or transmitted, in any form or by any means, electronic, mechanical, photocopying, recording or otherwise, without the prior permission of the publisher or the Copyright Licensing Agency.

Bible and other acknowledgments can be found on pages 111–12.

First published 2020

British Library Cataloguing-in-Publication Data
A catalogue record for this book is available from the British Library.

ISBN: 978–1–78974–163–6
eBook ISBN: 978–1–78974–164–3

Set in Avenir 11/15pt
Typeset in Great Britain by CRB Associates, Potterhanworth, Lincolnshire
Printed in Great Britain by 4edge Limited

Inter-Varsity Press publishes Christian books that are true to the Bible and that communicate the gospel, develop discipleship and strengthen the church for its mission in the world.

IVP originated within the Inter-Varsity Fellowship, now the Universities and Colleges Christian Fellowship, a student movement connecting Christian Unions in universities and colleges throughout Great Britain, and a member movement of the International Fellowship of Evangelical Students. Website: www.uccf.org.uk. That historic association is maintained, and all senior IVP staff and committee members subscribe to the UCCF Basis of Faith.

Contributors

Nehemiah 8:1–18 and Habakkuk 1:1–11; 3:16–19
Jonathan Lamb
Jonathan is Minister-at-Large for Keswick Ministries. He was previously CEO of Keswick Ministries and Director of Langham Preaching. He is the author of a number of books, including *Preaching Matters: Encountering the living God* and *Integrity: Leading with God watching* (IVP, 2014 and 2006, respectively). He also serves as a Vice President of IFES (International Fellowship of Evangelical Students).

Psalms 1 and 19
Alistair Begg
Alistair has been Senior Pastor at Parkside Church, Ohio, since 1983. He is the voice behind the daily radio broadcast *Truth for Life* and has written a number of books. His most recent one is *Pray Big* (The Good Book Company, 2019).

Psalm 32
John Risbridger
John is the Minister and Team Leader at Above Bar Church in Southampton. He served as Chair of Keswick Ministries

and is now Council Chair of the Evangelical Alliance. He wrote *The Message of Worship* (2015) in IVP's Bible Speaks Today series.

Psalms 97, 98 and 100
Alec Motyer

Alec Motyer was Vice-Principal of Clifton Theological College and Vicar of St Luke's, Hampstead, before becoming Principal of Trinity College, Bristol. He was much loved on both sides of the Atlantic as a Bible expositor and a prolific author.

John 16:1–33
Peter Maiden

Peter Maiden retired from the role of International Director of Operation Mobilisation and became International Director Emeritus, a role offering more time for preaching and teaching in the UK and worldwide. He also serves Keswick Ministries as Minister-at-Large. He is the author of a number of books, including *Discipleship Matters* and *Radical Gratitude*.

Romans 5:1–11
Stuart Briscoe

Stuart was the Senior Pastor of Elmbrook Church in Wisconsin for thirty years. He has written more than forty books and continues to broadcast daily worldwide via *Telling the Truth* media ministry. He is now Minister-at-Large for Elmbrook Church.

Galatians 5:16–26
Derek Tidball

Derek served as the pastor of two Baptist churches and as the Principal of the London School of Theology for twelve years. He now teaches in various colleges, including Spurgeon's, Moorlands and SAIACS (Bangalore). He has written many books, including a number of commentaries in IVP's Bible Speaks Today series.

Philippians 1:1–11
Paul Mallard

Paul has worked in churches in Chippenham, Worcester and Birmingham and was FIEC President from 2004 to 2007. He has written a number of books, including *Invest Your Suffering* and *Invest Your Disappointments*. He is now Senior Pastor of Widcombe Baptist Church in Bath.

James 1:1–8
Michael Baughen

Michael served as Rector of Holy Trinity Church in Platt Lane, Rusholme, Manchester and at All Souls, Langham Place in London, before becoming the Bishop of Chester.

Following his retirement, he worked as an honorary assistant bishop in the Diocese of London and in the Diocese of Southwark. He is also a hymn writer.

1 Peter 1:1–12
Don Carson
Don Carson is Research Professor of New Testament at Trinity Evangelical Divinity School in Deerfield, Illinois. He has written more than fifty books, serves on several boards and is a guest lecturer in academic and church settings around the world. Along with Tim Keller, he founded The Gospel Coalition.

1 Peter 4:12–19
Donald English
Donald English taught New Testament in Nigeria, Manchester and Bristol. He also served as a minister in two churches in the north-east of England. Twice he was elected President of the Methodist Conference. His last appointment was leading the Methodist Home Mission Division. In 1996, he was awarded a CBE.

1 John 1:1–10
Steve Brady
Steve held four pastorates in the UK before serving as Principal of Moorlands College. He has spoken at

conferences and conventions around the world, many linked to the UK Keswick Convention, of which he was a trustee for two decades. He is now the Senior Pastor at First Baptist Church, Grand Cayman.

Preface

What is the collective name for a group of preachers? A troop, a gaggle, a chatter, a pod . . . ? I'm not sure! But in this Food for the Journey series, we have gathered an excellent group of Bible teachers to help us unpack the Scriptures and understand some of the core issues every Christian needs to know and understand.

Each book is based on a particular theme and contains excerpts from messages given by much-loved Keswick Convention speakers, past and present. Where necessary, the language has been updated, but, on the whole, this is what you would have heard had you been listening in the tent on Skiddaw Street. A wide, though not exhaustive, selection of Bible passages explore the key theme, and each day of the devotional ends with a fresh section of application designed to help you apply God's Word to your own life and situation.

Whether you are a Convention regular or have never been to Keswick, this Food for the Journey series is a unique opportunity to study the Scriptures and a particular topic with a range of gifted Bible teachers by your side. Each book is designed to fit in your jacket pocket or handbag so you can read it anywhere – over the breakfast table, on the commute into work or college, while you are waiting in your car, over your lunch break or in bed at night. Wherever life's journey takes you, time in God's Word is vital nourishment for your spiritual journey.

Our prayer is that these devotionals become your daily feast, a nourishing opportunity to meet with God through his Word. Read, meditate, apply and pray through the Scriptures given for each day, and allow God's truths to take root and transform your life.

If these devotionals whet your appetite for more, there is a 'For further study' section at the end of each book. You can also visit our website <www.keswickministries.org> to find the full range of books, study guides, CDs, DVDs and mp3s available.

Let the word of Christ dwell in you richly
(Colossians 3:16, ESV)

Rediscovering joy

The night before he died, Jesus had a final meal with his disciples. This was his last opportunity to prepare them for all that would follow, and he taught them many things – that he would come back, that he would send the Holy Spirit, that union with him was the only way to bear spiritual fruit.

But Jesus wasn't just conveying information. He said, 'I have told you this so that my joy may be in you and that your joy may be complete' (John 15:11). Jesus was approaching Calvary, his time on earth was short, and yet he was deeply concerned about his disciples' joy.

Was Jesus really expecting this soon-to-be-persecuted motley group of believers to be joyful after his departure? Does he really expect you and me to be joyful when we are blindsided by grief and weighed down by the responsibilities of life? It certainly seems so.

Jesus' priority of joy is a resounding theme throughout the Bible. The Israelites celebrated God's saving acts with joy, an angel announcing Jesus' birth was a cause for great joy, John the Baptist joyfully welcomed Jesus' ministry, the early church shared meals and worshipped together with joy, the Philippian jailer was filled with joy when he accepted the gospel, and Paul was overjoyed as he saw new converts growing in the faith.

What was their secret?

Perhaps we need to rediscover what joy really is. Joy is not an inane triumphalism, a spike in mood or a personality trait. It cannot be conjured up by good circumstances or extinguished by bad. It's not dependent on healthy bank accounts, well-adjusted children or a lack of trials. Indeed, the most joyful people are often well acquainted with suffering. Joy in the Bible is the consequence of grasping eternal certainties: we are loved by God the Father, redeemed by his Son, indwelt by his Spirit and headed for the new heavens and the new earth. Paul urges us in Philippians 4:4: 'Rejoice *in the Lord* always', and when we focus on him, we have infinite reasons to be joyful. Jesus is the source and sustainer of our joy. He is where joy finds its anchor, and there is no joy apart from him.

Joni Eareckson Tada is probably the most joyful person I have ever met. Her smile is captivating and belies the fact that she is severely disabled and confined to a wheelchair. On 30 July 1967, she was paralysed from the neck down when she dived into unexpectedly shallow water in Chesapeake Bay. For more than fifty years, she has suffered chronic pain and has had to rely on others doing the most basic and intimate tasks for her. She writes,

> And now, nearly fifty years later, I still find myself thinking, *how in the world did I ever make it?* But here I am, living in joyful hope . . . How did that happen? Here's how: day after day, month after month, year after year, I simply cast myself on Jesus. I clung to his name, crying out constantly, 'O Jesus!'
> (Joni Eareckson Tada, *A Spectacle of Glory*, Zondervan, 2016, p. 287)

The lives of Joni and countless others, including sufferers, back up what the Bible teaches: nothing can separate us from the love of Christ, so nothing can take away our joy – it is ours now and for eternity. Of course, many things can stifle our joy – busyness, guilt and bitterness are common culprits. But there is a way back. Joy can be recovered and cultivated if we refocus on Jesus, its source. Joy is not just a command, it's a fruit of the Spirit that blossoms as faith deepens. Today, you can begin the journey of rediscovering joy as you seek to trust God's sovereignty, believe his promises and obey his Word.

C. S. Lewis once famously said that joy is the 'serious business of heaven' (*Letters to Malcolm: Chiefly on Prayer*, HarperOne, 2017, p. 125). Let's make it the serious business of earth too.

> To him who is able to keep you from stumbling and to present you before his glorious presence without fault and with great joy – to the only God our Saviour be glory, majesty, power and authority, through Jesus Christ our Lord, before all ages, now and for evermore! Amen.
> (Jude 1:24–25)

Nehemiah

King Cyrus of Persia had allowed the Jewish exiles to return to Jerusalem. But when Nehemiah, cupbearer to King Artaxerxes, heard that almost 100 years later the city walls of his homeland had not been rebuilt, he was heartbroken. The King sent him to oversee the building project.

The book recounts the rebuilding of the wall, the opposition, the new residents chosen to live in the city, and Nehemiah's reforms. It describes the celebrations when people heard Ezra read the Law after the work had been complete – a reminder of the joy we can know today when we read and obey God's Word.

Day 1

Read Nehemiah 8:1–18
Key verses: Nehemiah 8:10, 12

....

Nehemiah said, 'Go and enjoy choice food and sweet drinks, and send some to those who have nothing prepared. This day is holy to our LORD. Do not grieve, for the joy of the LORD is your strength . . .' 12 Then all the people went away to eat and drink, to send portions of food and to celebrate with great joy, because they now understood the words that had been made known to them.

How did you feel the last time you read your Bible? Comforted, challenged, joyful . . . ?

In Nehemiah 8, the Israelites had finished rebuilding the walls of Jerusalem and had gathered in the square before the Water Gate to listen to Ezra the scribe reading from the 'Book of the Law of Moses' (verse 1). The first reading of the Law provoked within them a sense of contrition as they realized that their lives had failed to match up to God's standards. But, intriguingly, Ezra and Nehemiah moved quickly to stop the people from mourning their failures (verses 9–10). Instead, they wanted the Israelites to see the bigger picture of God's purpose, accept joyfully all that God had done for them and recall his grace.

So the people went off to celebrate, to eat and drink 'with great joy' (verse 12). After standing listening to God's Word from 'daybreak till noon' (verse 3), they must have headed off to the party with added zest! They were back home in Jerusalem and had finally come to realize, from all that had been read, that God's desire was to bless them: 'They now understood the words that had been made known to them' (verse 12). It was for this reason that the 'joy of the LORD' was their strength – the word means their 'fortress', their 'stronghold'. It is the awareness that God has good purposes for us, that his Law is for our benefit, and that his actions of mercy and grace are for our well-being, our shalom.

Full appreciation of that cannot fail to generate a deep sense of joy and thanksgiving in our lives too.

Today, remember that God is *for* you. The eternal, sovereign God wants to bless you. Daily, he showers you with grace and mercy, and is acting in many, often unseen, ways on your behalf. His greatest blessing was sending Christ to die in your place, for your sins. Ultimately, God's good purpose is to make you like Christ, and even now he is working to conform you into the image of his Son.

> The LORD is my strength and my shield;
>> my heart trusts in him, and he helps me.
> My heart leaps for joy,
>> and with my song I praise him.
> The LORD is the strength of his people,
>> a fortress of salvation for his anointed one.
> Save your people and bless your inheritance;
>> be their shepherd and carry them for ever.
> (Psalm 28:7–9)

Day 2

Read Nehemiah 8:1–18
Key verses: Nehemiah 8:17–18

··

The whole company that had returned from exile built temporary shelters and lived in them. From the days of Joshua son of Nun until that day, the Israelites had not celebrated it like this. And their joy was very great. [18] *Day after day, from the first day to the last, Ezra read from the Book of the Law of God. They celebrated the festival for seven days, and on the eighth day, in accordance with the regulation, there was an assembly.*

Have you noticed how often the Bible talks about celebrating?

On the second day of their Bible study no less, the Israelites discovered the Feast of Booths, a harvest festival, when they specially remembered deliverance from Egypt and the long march to the Promised Land (verses 13–14). So, just as it was written in Leviticus 23, they went out and built their shanty huts. For seven days, they were not only celebrating the liberation of God's people from Egypt, but also their own return from exile (verse 17). Notice that their joy was inclusive: they cared for those without resources and showed compassion to those in need (verse 10).

Believe it or not, joy should be the hallmark of true Christian faith. Of course, how we express it is sometimes to do with our personalities and our culture, and God respects that. But what have we done to provoke so many people to imagine that the Christian faith is so joyless? Before his conversion, Ernest Gordon, the author of *Miracle on the River Kwai*, thought of Christians as people who had 'managed to extract the bubbles from the champagne of life'. He said he would prefer 'a robust hell to this grey, sunless abode of the faithful' (quoted in *To End All Wars*, Zondervan, 2001, p. 115). I know that when people describe the church as boring, it says as much about them as the church. But so often, there is the missing dimension of celebration. I like the remark of the German pastor and theologian, Helmut Thielicke: 'Should we not see that lines of laughter about the eyes are just as much marks of faith as are the lines of care and seriousness?' (quoted by R. Kent Hughes, *James*, Crossway, 2015, p. 115).

God is particularly interested in our joy. He tells us, 'Be glad in the Lord, and rejoice, O righteous, and shout for joy, all you upright in heart!' (Psalm 32:11). When the church gathers, the sense of confident joy in God should be pronounced. When we fail to demonstrate delight and satisfaction in God, we're not only dishonoring God, we're disobeying Him. More than anyone else on earth, Christians have a reason to celebrate.

(Bob Kauflin, *Worship Matters*, Crossway, 2008, p. 167)

Consider how you could incorporate more God-focused celebrations into your church and family life. Make time for joy! Celebrate well!

Psalms

Imagine being able to sing the songs Jesus sang or pray the prayers he prayed.

Well, we can! Jesus, like many Israelites before and after him, used the Psalms in his public and private worship. The Psalms are collections of prayers and songs gathered over a number of centuries and written by a variety of authors, including King David. They are full of personal testimony, but direct our focus to God as King and Creator, Judge and Redeemer, Helper and Deliverer. Each psalm is carefully crafted poetry, rich in imagery, and, although written for a specific context, contains timeless truths. On any and every occasion, we can go to the Psalms and find words to express our emotions, words of Scripture we can use to speak to God.

Day 3

Read Psalm 1
Key verse: Psalm 1:1

....

Blessed is the one
  who does not walk in step with the wicked
or stand in the way that sinners take
  or sit in the company of mockers.

In every survey about what humans want out of life, you will find right at the very top of the list, or at least in the top five answers, that people of all ages will say, 'I would just like to be happy.' The pursuit of happiness and joy is relevant to every generation, and this psalm tells us how to find it.

'Blessed', or to put it another way, 'happy' or 'joyful', is the man or woman who 'does not walk in step with the wicked' (verse 1). Walking is a metaphor for lifestyle, and one that Paul frequently used: 'I urge you to walk in a manner worthy of the calling to which you have been called' (Ephesians 4:1, ESV). We need to read this psalm in the light of Paul's words. He is saying, 'You who are in Christ must no longer walk as the old man you were in Adam, because you are no longer the old man you once were.' And the practical expression of our new life in Christ will be displayed in the fact that we take our counsel, not from a world view that is alien to these things, but rather from the Word of God itself. We submit to the rule of the Lord Jesus and weed out everything that stands against his Word and his will.

The happy or joyful person does not 'stand in the way that sinners take'. That means we do not allow sinful thoughts, world views orientated without God, to shape our thinking and way of life. Notice that the three negatives in verse 1 are not simply parallel statements, but progressive: there is a downward spiral of sin. The devil is deceitful, seducing us little by little, sowing seeds of doubt in our minds. He then tempts us to take a stand in matters contrary to God's Word so that it becomes customary to our way of life. And then, if possible, he urges us to take a seat, establishing ourselves there.

What is the secret to happiness? Blessing attends those who are not taking counsel from the wicked, are not parking their car in the car park of the sinner, and are certainly not sitting down to scoff at the things we know we ought to hold dear.

The real secret of joy, the key to walking along the pathway of Psalm 1, is saying 'No' to what we should say no to, and saying 'Yes' to what we ought to say yes to. Pray for God's help and strength to do this today.

For the grace of God has appeared that offers salvation to all people. It teaches us to say 'No' to ungodliness and worldly passions, and to live self-controlled, upright and godly lives in this present age.

(Titus 2:11–12)

Day 4

Read Psalm 1
Key verses: Psalm 1:1–2

. . . .

> *Blessed is the one*
> *who does not walk in step with the wicked*
> *or stand in the way that sinners take*
> *or sit in the company of mockers,*
> *²but whose delight is in the law of the LORD,*
> *and who meditates on his law day and night.*

What is the secret to experiencing true joy?

Joy unfurls within us as we avoid sin (Day 3) and delight in God's Word. It is dependent on both these things. Verse 2: the individual's 'delight is in the law of the LORD'. The instructions of the law are a delight to this person. Delighting in the law of the Lord means that each part of my life is being brought into harmony with the Word and will of God. The people who are close to you will know that your life is increasingly being brought under the jurisdiction of Scripture, and delightfully so. And that delight leads to meditation 'on his law day and night'. This interest in God's Word is not just a passing fancy, it is not just a brief intrusion into the day or week. It is certainly not a twenty-minute talk once a week – it is far more significant than that.

Neither is the psalmist advocating Eastern meditative practices. Rather, he urges us to use our minds and bring our emotions once again into line with the truth of God's Word. The word 'meditate' is the same word translated 'plot' in Psalm 2. 'Why do the nations conspire and the peoples plot in vain?' (verse 1). In other words, why do they sit down and cogitate on what they could possibly do in order to undermine this king? You see, meditating is not something that causes us to sit quietly by ourselves, although there is great value in doing so. Rather, it is the thoughtful progression that leads to action. Think of Joshua, that man of action. You don't imagine him sitting around very much. What did God say to him? 'Keep this Book of the Law always on your lips; meditate on it day and night, so that you may be careful to do everything written in it' (Joshua 1:8).

Are you too busy for joy? With the relentless demands of our schedules and a never-ending 'to do' list, do we need to make a conscious decision to take time to 'delight' in God's Word? It is easy for our Bible reading to be like a fast-food snack rather than a gourmet meal. Try memorizing and meditating – chewing, cogitating on God's Word – so that your emotions are brought into line with God's truth and your behaviour reflects his will.

> When the early believers converted to Christ, it never occurred to them to fit Him into the margins of their busy lives. They redefined themselves around a new, immovable center. He was not an optional weekend activity, along with the kids' soccer practices. They put Him and His church and His cause first in their hearts, first in their schedules, first in their budgets, first in their reputations, first in their very lives. They devoted themselves [Acts 2:42].
>
> (Ray Ortlund, blog post, 16 February 2010, www.thegospelcoalition.org/blogs/ray-ortlund/they-devoted-themselves/)

Day 5

Read Psalm 1
Key verse: Psalm 1:3

....

*That person is like a tree planted by streams
    of water,
  which yields its fruit in season
and whose leaf does not wither –
  whatever they do prospers.*

If you had to paint a picture of what joy looks like, what would you paint?

The illustration in Psalm 1:3 comes pretty close with this image of the divine Gardener who plants and provides the irrigation essential for fruitfulness. The verse reminds us of Jesus' words: 'You did not choose me, but I chose you and appointed you so that you might go and bear fruit – fruit that will last' (John 15:16).

But there are seasons of fruitfulness. Our souls are not always in the full bloom of summer. Sometimes we look round and are envious at the prosperity of the wicked (Psalm 73:3). People who are not remotely interested in God, ignoring all the instructions in this psalm, seem to be prospering immensely. We, in turn, try our best to live under the rule of his law, joyfully obey his Word, and it certainly doesn't seem as if we are prospering. But from the perspective of eternity and viewed from the vantage point of the assembly of God, Psalm 73 explains what is really going on. Many things come into our lives that do not immediately fit with the notion of prospering, but the righteous will prosper, because the only prosperity that really matters is found on the pathway of God's appointing.

Ultimately, the wicked will perish. They will not be able to stand before the judging gaze of God. On that day, he will administer his fair and final judgment (Psalm 1:4–5). But for those who turn to the Lord now, there is mercy and salvation (Isaiah 55:6–7). There is also the promise: 'the LORD knows the way of the righteous' (Psalm 1:6 ESV). Psalm 139 explains that he knows when you sit down, when you stand up. He knows the words of your mouth before you even speak them. He has a whole universe to care for, and yet he knows you. Amazing!

Who can live Psalm 1 perfectly? Only Jesus. Who lives in perfect community with the Father? Only the Son. Who is it that delights in the Word of God and prospers? Jesus.

In Christ, you may become a blessed, happy, joyful person, because he has fulfilled all the demands of the law, he has paid the penalty for all our sin, and he grants us his righteousness so that we, living in union with him, discover that our way is known to the Lord. Paul says, 'you are in Christ Jesus, who has become for us wisdom from God – that is, our righteousness, holiness and redemption. Therefore, as it is written: "Let the one who boasts boast in the Lord"' (1 Corinthians 1:30–31).

> If Christians do not rejoice, it is not because they are Christians, but because they are not Christian enough. Joy is the rational state of the Christian in view of his [or her] spiritual position in Christ.
> (Derek Prime and Alistair Begg, *On Being a Pastor*, Moody Press, 2013, p. 52)

Day 6

Read Psalm 19
Key verses: Psalm 19:7–8

....

The law of the LORD is perfect,
  refreshing the soul.
The statutes of the LORD are trustworthy,
  making wise the simple.
⁸*The precepts of the LORD are right,*
  giving joy to the heart.
The commands of the LORD are radiant,
  giving light to the eyes.

In our culture of fake news, people find themselves asking, 'Can we trust anything we read?'

Here, the psalmist, David, says that you can trust the law of the Lord, because it is perfect, without flaw or error, and it is absolutely and directly suited to the needs of those who read it. The word for 'law' is a comprehensive term, essentially to do with everything God has revealed of himself. It involves not only the law itself, but also the prophets and the psalms. It wouldn't be wrong for us to read simply, 'The Word of the Lord is perfect.'

Scan your eyes down the words used to describe God's law in verses 7 and 8: perfect, trustworthy, right and radiant. These are synonyms. David is deliberately piling up these words that have the same meaning in order to drive home the value of the Scriptures and the need to obey them. Let's look at one phrase: 'The precepts of the LORD are right, giving joy to the heart.' Does reading the Bible fill you with joy?

People are searching for happiness and contentment in our world. The progress promised by the humanism of the past three centuries is now gravely threatened by an understanding of the human person that reduces our humanity to a cosmic chemical accident. If humanity has no intentional origin, if God didn't create us, then there is no ultimate destiny or way to make sense of life. Materialism – and all the other isms too – leave us high and dry. In contrast, the Bible, if you really understand its message, fills you with unspeakable joy.

David is saying, here is God's Word that has been given to you. It is perfect, it converts, revives and brings life. It is reliable testimony – you can base your life on it and it will make you wise. It is absolutely right. It brings joy to the heart and enlightens the eyes. In other words, the Bible shows us what we must believe. The precepts tell us what we need to do. The warnings tell us what we need to avoid. And the promises tell us what we are able to hope for and to trust.

Heavenly Father, help me learn to love your Word. In reading and studying it, revive, guide and keep me. Captivate my heart, mind and consciousness by its truth. In the pages of the written Word, reveal the Living Word, the Lord Jesus Christ. Help me to be able to say with the psalmist of your words:

They are more precious than gold,
    than much pure gold;
they are sweeter than honey,
    than honey from the honeycomb.
(Psalm 19:10)

Day 7

Read Psalm 32
Key verses: Psalm 32:1–2

....

Blessed is the one
 whose transgressions are forgiven,
 whose sins are covered.
2 Blessed is the one
 whose sin the Lord does not count against them
 and in whose spirit is no deceit.

What has a cover-up got to do with joy?

Psalm 32 is all about a cover-up. The context is most likely the time that King David seduced another man's wife while her husband was at war. Her name was Bathsheba, and David even went as far as arranging for her husband to be killed in battle so he could have her for himself (2 Samuel 11).

This massive cover-up of sin was destroying David. Psalm 32:3–4 describe him wasting away. His strength, joy, self-respect and energy were diminishing.

Relief only came when he confessed his sin and found that God was not harsh and vindictive, but full of grace and compassion (verse 5). It was the joy of knowing this forgiveness that led David to write this psalm. You could translate 'blessed' from verses 1 and 2 as 'happy'. He wanted others to know: 'What joy for those whose disobedience is forgiven' (verse 1, NLT). This joy is for all those 'in whose spirit is no deceit' (verse 2). David is not talking about perfect people, but about those who have confessed their sin to God and are no longer lying about it or covering it up.

When we confess our sins, we too find God's forgiveness is not conditional, lukewarm, distant, a concession somehow squeezed out of him reluctantly. It is total and unqualified. Because Jesus has dealt with your sins on the cross, they are not on your shoulders any more. He's covered over all their shame and paid the penalty for ever, so there is nothing left for you to pay. God has made you righteous in Christ. You are blessed, you're loved, you're family, you're free. That's the outrageous grace of God – no wonder we can be joyful.

The God whom David feared would expose and condemn him now surrounds him with songs of deliverance (verse 5). It may be that David is talking generally about God's protection, but the link with the previous verses is so strong that when we read about the rising flood waters, we should be recalling the great flood Noah experienced in Genesis 6. Those waters were an expression of God's judgment. Just as Noah, who trusted God, was protected from judgment through the Ark, lifted up above the flood water and saved, so we too are protected from the judgment of God as we ask for his forgiveness, open up the dark places of our lives to him, and trust ourselves to Christ for his mercy and protection.

David's urgent plea is for us to find the joy of forgiveness while there is still time: the opportunity won't last for ever.

Today, confess your sins to God, receive his gracious forgiveness, and know the joy of a renewed relationship with your heavenly Father.

Repentance that renews precious fellowship with our incomparably wonderful God ultimately furthers our joy. Just as we cannot enter into true repentance without sorrow for our guilt, we cannot emerge from true repentance without joy for release from shame.
(Bryan Chapell, *Holiness by Grace*, Crossway, 2011, p. 88)

Day 8

Read Psalm 97
Key verses: Psalm 97:1–2

....

The Lord reigns, let the earth be glad;
*   let the distant shores rejoice.*
2Clouds and thick darkness surround him;
*   righteousness and justice are the foundation*
*   of his throne.*

Is it possible to be truly joyful when our loved ones aren't Christians?

It is difficult to rejoice when we think of the judgment that is in store for them. Yet, strangely, in verses 1 and 2, we have joy co-existing with condemnation. In verse 1, the earth rejoices because God is King and, without any link, verse 2 gives us a picture of God's throne when he came to his people at Mount Sinai (Exodus 19). The darkness and smoke demonstrate his righteousness and justice, and portray the threatening, judgmental side of the holiness of God. Here is true joy existing alongside an earth that melts when the Lord appears.

Verses 3–5 speak of God's presence bringing destruction. 'Fire goes before him' – fire is the symbol of the holiness of God, and especially his antagonism to sin. Remember when Mount Sinai was surrounded by smoke because the Lord had descended on it in fire? The people were not allowed to approach because God had warned: 'Put limits around the mountain and set it apart as holy' (Exodus 19:23). In verse 5, the mountains melted like wax. Why? What did the Lord do? Well, he didn't do anything. He just came. The mere presence of God, and the whole physical fabric of the world begins to disintegrate.

One day, the preaching of the gospel will be finished. The sense of the Hebrew text in verses 6–7 is of a completed act: the word has gone round the whole world. God speaks, in verse 7, of a universal opportunity that has been given, and a merited judgment. Everyone who has refused to give God their loyalty reaps the shame they deserved. The gods they have worshipped will also bow before God.

Zion now rejoices in judgment (verse 8). At the end of time, there will be those who fall under God's judgment. And yet, somehow, the joy of God's people will be undimmed. Verse 9 adds a word of explanation: 'For you, LORD, are the Most High over all the earth.' The people of God will be caught up in the vision of the glory of the supremacy of their God, who is most high over all the earth, and exalted far above all gods. This doesn't take away the mystery, but it goes far to explaining the joy.

You may wonder how you could possibly experience joy in eternity if your loved ones weren't with you. Today we weep, all the while praying that the Holy Spirit will open their eyes to the truth of the gospel and give us opportunities to witness and model Christ to them. But when God has completed his work, there will be no more tears, and our focus will be trained on him. We will be caught up in the vision of the glory of the supremacy of our God; rejoicing in his righteousness, justice and holiness. Praise the Lord!

Day 9

Read Psalm 97
Key verses: Psalm 97:10–12

....

Let those who love the LORD hate evil,
    for he guards the lives of his faithful ones
    and delivers them from the hand of the wicked.
11 Light shines on the righteous
    and joy on the upright in heart.
12 Rejoice in the LORD, you who are righteous,
    and praise his holy name.

Jesus is coming again. Those who 'love the LORD' have to get ready for this final day.

How should we prepare? The psalmist advises us thus.

• Hate evil (verse 10)

  When Jesus returns and establishes the new heavens and the new earth, his abhorrence of sin will be un-mistakable. Ephesians 5:5 makes it clear that evil will have no place in 'the kingdom of Christ and of God'. In the meantime, we must hate evil too. Our ethics, our moral principles, must derive their strength and con-. viction from what God will do on the last day. 2 Peter 3:11–12 makes the same point: 'Since everything will be destroyed in this way, what kind of people ought you to be? You ought to live holy and godly lives as you look forward to the day of God and speed its coming.' When we commit ourselves to God and his values, he in turn commits himself to us. His preserving grace guarantees our perseverance, and rescues us from every enemy.

• Rejoice in the Lord (verse 12)

Be joyful as you remember God's holiness. The psalmist urges us to remember the name of God and the meaning of that name, which indicates the kind of God he is (Exodus 3:15). In the realities and difficulties of life, we are joyfully to remember that God is our deliverer and redeemer, and commit ourselves to him.

• Believe his faithful promises (verse 11)

The essence of verse 11 is: 'Light is sown for the right-eous, and gladness for the upright in heart.' I think the translators took fright because they have never sown light in their gardens. But God is not afraid of mixing his metaphors! Sowing looks forward to the reaping of a crop. Light stands for all that is joyous, all that relieves,

DAY 9 | **31**

all that uplifts. God has *planted* it. And the day will
come when God's righteous ones will reap the crop. In
the meantime, as we wait for his coming, we rest on the
promise that our joy is secure, and one day our salvation
will be complete.

The events of the final day are as certain as if they had
already happened. The joy we will experience in the
new heavens and the new earth is a sure promise to
cling to. In the meantime, as we live holy lives, we can
find joy in God himself. Today, rejoice in God's great
name and all that it signifies.

There exists a delight that is not given to the wicked,
but to those honouring Thee, O God, without desiring
recompense, the joy of whom Thou art Thyself! And this
is a blessed life, to rejoice towards Thee, about thee,
for Thy sake.
(Augustine, *Confessions* X, 32, quoted in John Piper,
When I Don't Desire God, Crossway, 2018, p. 18)

Let all who take refuge in you be glad;
    let them ever sing for joy.
Spread your protection over them,
    that those who love your name may rejoice in you.
(Psalm 5:11)

Day 10

Read Psalm 98
Key verse: Psalm 98:1

....

Sing to the Lord a new song,
for he has done marvellous things;
his right hand and his holy arm
have worked salvation for him.

Psalm 98 is a call to joy. It rests on three exhortations. Verse 1: 'sing to the Lord a new song.' Verse 4: 'Shout for joy to the Lord, all the earth'. Verse 7: 'Let the sea resound.' Three great invitations to make an enormous noise!

The first exhortation is to be joyful because of our salvation. God has accomplished salvation (verse 1). It's a salvation that only he could have achieved: '*his* right hand and *his* holy arm have worked salvation for *him*'. Salvation begins in the mind of God: it is something he wants. It is done by his personal agency, 'his right hand', in keeping with his character. God doesn't wait for us to realize our need for salvation. He diagnoses the problem and provides the remedy. In verse 3, God has 'remembered' – salvation originates in God's unprovoked love, a love we could never have imagined or deserved. It has welled up in God's heart because he is like that. God's love was first for 'Israel', but its ultimate objective is the whole world: 'all the ends of the earth have seen the salvation of our God.' We can experience deep joy today when we trust in this divine, finished work of salvation.

The second exhortation invites us to 'Shout for joy to the King' (verses 4–6). The Lord's kingship is a source of joyful praise.

The third exhortation is: 'Let the sea resound'. Why? 'For he comes' (verse 9). Our joy will be completed by the coming of the Lord. At last, it's not just the sea and creation praising God, but a redeemed humanity using harps, voices, trumpets, horns – all means – to offer a great paean of praise. Today, the church – the fruit of the gospel – is full of people ready to roar out their appreciation 'before the LORD, the King'.

Whatever trials or difficulties you face, you can rejoice because of your salvation, because God is King, and because Jesus is returning. Today, turn up the volume on the worship songs and sing with heartfelt praise: 'Shout for joy before the LORD, the King . . . sing before the LORD, for he comes' (Psalm 98:6, 9).

> I will sing the LORD's praise, for he has been good
> to me.
> (Psalm 13:6)

> I will sing of the LORD's great love for ever;
> with my mouth I will make your faithfulness known
> through all generations.
> (Psalm 89:1)

> Come, let us sing for joy to the LORD;
> let us shout aloud to the Rock of our salvation.
> Let us come before him with thanksgiving
> and extol him with music and song.
> (Psalm 95:1–2)

Day 11

Read Psalm 100
Key verses: Psalm 100:1–2

....

*Shout for joy to the L*ORD*, all the earth.*
*²Worship the L*ORD *with gladness;*
come before him with joyful songs.

Have you ever wondered what songs Jesus would have sung?

No doubt Psalm 100 would have been a favourite. It invites all people on the earth to worship the Lord with gladness, because he is God and because he is good. The Israelites sang this psalm in the temple. Subsequently it was part and parcel of the worship within the synagogue services. And now, the choirmaster, as it were, invites us to add our voices to the crowd of singers.

Psalm 100 provides a climax to a series of psalms that extol God's kingship, and it is right that we should celebrate God's sovereignty with joyful praise. Amazingly, this

King welcomes us into his presence. In verses 1–2, we have three commands or invitations, each indicating increasing access to God: 'Shout', 'Worship', 'Come before him'. We shout out from afar, we worship him, and then we come right to where he is. We come and stand before him. The people of God are welcomed into the presence of God.

And we come joyfully. Why? Because of what God has done for us. He has 'made us' (verse 3). This is a reference not to creation, but to redemption. We who were formerly sinners have now become the redeemed people of God. If that were not cause enough for rejoicing, God is our shepherd, we are his people, the sheep of his pasture. We look forward and see him as God; backwards and see the work of salvation he has accomplished; and around, to see his shepherding care. And we rejoice that we belong to him.

The second half of the psalm invites us to come nearer into the presence of God. 'Enter his gates . . . and his courts', and then 'give thanks' and 'praise his name'. We praise God for who he is. Verse 5 declares, 'The LORD is good and his love endures for ever; his faithfulness continues through all generations.' We look at him and see that he is essentially, wholly, completely, utterly good. We look at him in his unvarying attitude to us and learn that his steadfast love is everlasting. We look at our experience of life and find that God's faithfulness, his reliability, just goes on and on.

This psalm is completely God-centred and a reminder that joy isn't dependent on circumstances or feelings, but rather is rooted in God himself and all that he has done for us – past, present and future. Consequently, our joy is in proportion to our God-centredness:

We minimize our joy when we neglect the daily worship of God in private. It is one of the great blessings of life that God does not limit our access to Him and enjoyment of His presence to only one day per week! Every day, the strength, guidance, encouragement, forgiveness, joy and all that God is, awaits us.

(Donald Whitney, *Spiritual Disciplines for the Christian Life*, NavPress, 2014, p. 113)

Habakkuk

We don't often get an insight into a prophet's private prayer life. But in the book of Habakkuk, we see the prophet crying out to God.

Habakkuk was a contemporary of Jeremiah and lived in Jerusalem. Under King Jehoiakim, wickedness, violence and anarchy were rife and the prophet couldn't understand why God did not intervene. When God answered his prayer and told him judgment would come through the hands of the evil Babylonians, Habakkuk was even more stunned. What changed the questions of 'Why?' and 'How long, Lord?' in chapter 1 to the worship of chapter 3? When God doesn't answer our prayers as we had hoped, when we don't understand what he is doing, how can we say with Habakkuk, 'Yet I will rejoice in the LORD, I will be joyful in God my Saviour'? (3:18).

Day 12

Read Habakkuk 1:1–11; 3:16-19
Key verses: Habakkuk 3:17–18

....

Though the fig-tree does not bud
and there are no grapes on the vines,
though the olive crop fails
and the fields produce no food,
though there are no sheep in the sheepfold
and no cattle in the stalls,
18yet I will rejoice in the LORD,
I will be joyful in God my Saviour.

Everything has gone.

It is possible that Habakkuk is anticipating the ultimate Day of the Lord. But it is also highly likely that he is referring to the devastating impact of the predicted invasion of the Babylonians described in chapter 1. This was the judgment God had promised because his people refused to obey him. Verse 17 begins with the apparent luxuries of figs, grapes and olives, but moves very quickly to show that there is no food at all. Habakkuk is describing not simply a devastated economic and social infrastructure, but total destruction.

That's what makes this small word 'yet' all the more remarkable. Habakkuk is stripped of everything, but still this man of faith sings, 'Yet I will rejoice in the LORD' (verse 18). How can Habakkuk respond as he does? What was there left for him to rejoice in? It was not his possessions; it was certainly not his circumstances. Like Job, he was stripped of everything but God. And that is the key to his joy: it is finding that God the Creator, the Redeemer, the covenant-keeping God is enough.

When we become Christians, we are not protected from the hardships of the world. There is no guarantee that we will be immune from suffering or from God's discipline, from the oppression of enemies, or from the pains and dangers of living in this broken world. But we know that the Lord will not let go of his people, that he has not abandoned his world. He is still in control, and his purposes will be fulfilled. People of faith have discovered that Habakkuk's song rings true. When everything is taken away, we can still say, 'I will rejoice in God.'

It is relatively easy to be joyful when we are healthy, our careers are on track, we're enjoying our retirement, our children are happy, and our marriages are fulfilling. But when you face life's uncertainties and turbulence, will you respond like Habakkuk, 'Yet I will rejoice in the LORD, I will be joyful in God my Saviour'? When everything you have come to rely on is stripped away, will you acknowledge that God is enough?

Observe, it is our duty and privilege to rejoice in God, and to rejoice in Him always; at all times, in all conditions; even when we suffer for Him, or are afflicted by Him. We must not think the worse of Him or of His ways for the hardships we meet with in His service. There is enough in God to furnish us with matter of joy in the worst circumstance on earth . . . Joy in God is a duty of great consequence in the Christian life; and Christians need to be again and again called to it.

(Matthew Henry, *Philippians*, CreateSpace Publishing, 2015, p. 60)

John

John, 'the disciple whom Jesus loved' (13:23), wrote this Gospel. The purpose for his eyewitness testimony of Jesus' life and ministry was 'that you may believe that Jesus is the Messiah, the Son of God, and that by believing you may have life in his name' (20:31). Chapters 12 – 19 focus exclusively on Jesus' last week – his final teaching, his prayers for his disciples and all believers, as well as his trial and crucifixion. Strangely, despite his imminent departure and the increasing persecution of his followers, Jesus promised his disciples joy. He promises the same joy to us, a joy that no one can take away.

Day 13

Read John 16:1–33
Key verse: John 16:7

....

But very truly I tell you, it is for your good that I am going away. Unless I go away, the Advocate will not come to you; but if I go, I will send him to you.

How can we experience the joy of Jesus when everything seems to be against us?

As we have discovered, in Scripture joy is much more than an emotion. It is a spiritual quality, grounded on God himself, and it comes from our relationship with him (Psalm 16:11; Philippians 4:4). Joy is also one of the fruits born in our lives, through the ministry of the Holy Spirit (Galatians 5:22–23). It is for me that deep underlying shalom peace; that deep sense of well-being; the assurance that a sovereign God has his hand upon my life, and that his Son has won eternal salvation for me; that I am 'in Christ', for ever united with him.

Jesus promised his disciples peace and joy (John 16:22, 33). This seemed an outrageous promise, given that he had just told them that greater persecution was on its way. They would be put out of the synagogue, ostracized from society and killed for their faith (verse 2). The disciples' fear and uncertainty is magnified when Jesus tells them he is leaving: 'It is for your good that I am going away' (verse 7).

You can imagine their confusion, even anger. 'You've just explained to us the struggles that we're about to face, and now you're walking out on us. How can that possibly be to our advantage?' Jesus replies, 'Unless I go away, the Advocate will not come to you; but if I go, I will send him to you.' Jesus must go away through death and resurrection to the glory of the Father's presence. Then he'll send the Holy Spirit. In sending the Holy Spirit, he will usher in the powers of the promised kingdom of God in the world.

In his address on the day of Pentecost, Peter explained the coming of the Holy Spirit. Objecting to the suggestion that the disciples were drunk, he said: 'No, this is what was spoken by the prophet Joel: "In the last days, God says, I will pour out my Spirit on all people"' (Acts 2:16–17).

That's how my Saviour, my Friend, walks with me and you, through the dark times as well as the good. He does so in the person of the Holy Spirit. Despite the hardships and pressures they were experiencing, the Holy Spirit – the ever-present God – was a source of joy for the disciples, and he can be for us too.

The day we trusted in Christ, we received the Holy Spirit. He helps us live the Christian life, grow in Christ-likeness, and persevere through suffering. He is God's presence with us – a constant source of love, joy and peace.

Today, thank God for the gift of his Spirit. Pray that his presence may be increasingly evident in your life and that you may follow his leading (Galatians 5:22–25).

> True joy comes only from God, and He shares this joy with those who walk in fellowship with Him.
> (Jerry Bridges, *The Pursuit of Holiness*, NavPress, 2016, p. 124)

Day 14

Read John 16:1–33
Key verses: John 16:16, 22

···

*Jesus went on to say, 'In a little while you will see me
no more, and then after a little while you will see
me. ²². . . now is your time of grief, but I will see you
again and you will rejoice, and no one will take away
your joy.*

'They worshiped together at the Temple each day, met in
homes for the Lord's Supper, and shared their meals with
great joy and generosity' (Acts 2:46, NLT). What changed
the grief of John 16 to the joy of Acts 2?

In John 16, Jesus knew the disciples were suffering, but
he was clear: 'You will see me no more, and then after a
little while you will see me . . . and no one will take away
your joy.' What does Jesus mean when he says, 'in a little
while you will see me no more'? Interpreters are divided
over whether 'the little while' refers to his second coming

or to the resurrection. I lean to the view that he's referring to the resurrection, but both these statements are true. Verse 22 also seems to be referring to the resurrection.

What transformed the early Christians' grief into joy? How can we have such a joy that no power on earth can take it away? The answer is that Jesus is alive. Our joy is based on events that have happened in history, and that can never be reversed. Jesus has defeated death and sin, and his resurrection has set in motion a chain of events that no power on earth can stop. In 1 Corinthians 15, Paul explains that Christ's resurrection is only the beginning. He is 'the first fruits of those who have fallen asleep'. When he returns, those who belong to him will be made alive. Then, the next step in this inevitable process is that the end will come when he hands over the kingdom to God the Father, and God is 'all in all' (1 Corinthians 15:28). Paul says the resurrection of Christ has sealed this. There can be no turning back. A process has been set in motion which nothing and no one can thwart, and it ends in final, glorious and complete victory. The reality of the resurrection and the hope of final victory mean that, despite intense struggles, no one can take away our joy.

I am the Living One; I was dead, and now look, I am alive for ever and ever! And I hold the keys of death and Hades.
(Revelation 1:18)

Jesus' resurrection defeated sin and death (1 Corinthians 15:54–57). He now lives in 'the power of an indestructible life' (Hebrews 7:16) and guarantees our eternal life (John 11:25–26). If he can never die and we can never die, then we will never be cut off from the source for our joy: Jesus.

This huge, breathtaking promise of never-ending joy is the joy of being with Jesus. No hardships, no suffering, not even our physical death, can separate us from Christ, so our joy can never be taken away.

Thanks be to God for his indescribable gift!
(2 Corinthians 9:15)

Day 15

Read John 16:1–33
Key verses: John 16:23–24, 26–27

....

In that day you will no longer ask me anything . . . my Father will give you whatever you ask in my name. ²⁴Until now you have not asked for anything in my name. Ask and you will receive, and your joy will be complete . . . ²⁶In that day you will ask in my name. I am not saying that I will ask the Father on your behalf. ²⁷No, the Father himself loves you because you have loved me and have believed that I came from God.

You weren't created for boredom or burnout or bondage to sexual lust or greed or ambition, but for the incomparable pleasure and matchless joy that knowing Jesus alone can bring. Only then, in Him, will you encounter the life-changing, thirst-quenching, soul-satisfying delight that God, for His glory, created you to experience.
(Sam Storms, *One Thing*, Christian Focus, 2010, p. 12)

Satan is a brilliant thief. He loves to rob us of the joy that Jesus died to purchase for us. He feeds us lies, and delights to distract us from the joy of a personal relationship with God the Father.

In verses 26–27, Jesus is talking about what this new, direct, intimate relationship with the Father looks like. In the name of Jesus, we can enter the presence of the One who loves us. Jesus encourages us to do this: 'Until now you have not asked for anything in my name. Ask and you will receive, and your joy will be complete.' Up until this point, the disciples had brought their requests directly to Jesus. But after his death and resurrection, he would remove the barrier of sin. From then on, with utter confidence, they could address the Father directly through Jesus, sure of the Father's love for them.

Not only can we speak directly to the Father, but he speaks to us. In verse 13, Jesus promises his disciples, 'When . . . the Spirit of truth comes, he will guide you into all the truth.' This was to be one of the special ministries of the Holy Spirit. It is a promise we must primarily apply to the apostles, and the books of the New Testament are the result of this promise. It's the promise of special, unique inspiration for the apostles to deliver the New Testament Scriptures to the people of God. Through all the ups and downs of life, as we move to the inevitable final victory of our Lord Jesus Christ, we have the wonderful companionship of the Holy Spirit, using Scripture to reveal more and more of the majesty of our God to us.

Don't let Satan rob you of the true joy that only comes from a relationship with God. Be intentional about cultivating this relationship, meeting God in his Word and through prayer.

The preservation of our joy in God takes work. It is a fight. Our adversary the devil prowls around like a roaring lion, and he has an insatiable appetite to destroy one thing: the joy of faith. But the Holy Spirit has given us a sword called the Word of God for the defense of our joy. Or, to change the image, when Satan huffs and puffs and tries to blow out the flame of your joy, you have an endless supply of kindling in the Word of God. (John Piper, *Desiring God*, Multnomah Press, 2011, p. 144)

Day 16

Read John 16:1–33
Key verse: John 16:28

....

*I came from the Father and entered the world; now I
am leaving the world and going back to the Father.*

What is the core reason for our joy?

The answer is found in the simplicity of verse 28. It is
almost a summary of Jesus' whole mission. 'I came from
the Father' – his virgin birth, his incarnation. 'I entered the
world' – his identification with us, his ministry among us.
'Now I am leaving the world and going back [by way of
the cross] to the Father.' That phrase 'back to the Father'
emphasizes the victory. His statement of what will happen,
step by step, is further evidence of his absolute control of
the situation. As Jesus said, when he spoke of dying and
giving his life for us, 'No one takes it from me, but I lay it
down of my own accord. I have authority to lay it down
and authority to take it up again. This command I received
from my Father' (John 10:18).

Our joy is that we know that everything Jesus came to do, he did perfectly and completely. On our good days, we can't add to our salvation; on our bad days, we can't subtract from it. Our salvation has been perfectly, completely secured by Christ's work on the cross. That's why Paul can write in Romans 8:1, 'There is now no condemnation for those who are in Christ Jesus.'

We are not appealing for mindless triumphalism. We need to be very real about our struggles (as we've already seen). Living for Christ involves struggles. There are many things that happen to us, or to those whom we love, that we can't understand or explain. But the knowledge that Christ himself has secured our ultimate salvation is surely the key to our joy.

> I delight greatly in the LORD;
>   my soul rejoices in my God.
> For he has clothed me with garments of salvation
>   and arrayed me in a robe of his righteousness.
> (Isaiah 61:10)

Christ was all anguish that I might be all joy, cast off that I might be brought in, trodden down as an enemy that I might be welcomed as a friend, surrendered to hell's worst that I might attain heaven's best, stripped that I might be clothed, wounded that I might be healed, athirst that I might drink, tormented that I might be comforted, made a shame that I might inherit glory, entered darkness that I might have eternal light. My Saviour wept that all tears might be wiped from my eyes, groaned that I might have endless song, endured all pain that I might have unfading health, bore a thorned crown that I might have a glory-diadem, bowed his head that I might uplift mine, experienced reproach that I might receive welcome, closed his eyes in death that I might gaze on unclouded brightness, expired that I might for ever live.

(Arthur Bennett, ed., *The Valley of Vision*, Banner of Truth, 1975, p. 42)

Romans and Galatians

The apostle Paul was a prolific letter writer. He wrote to churches and individuals on a variety of issues. His letters to the Romans and Galatians focus around the core truths of the gospel, and in this context, he explains the joy all Christians can experience.

Romans

Paul had always longed to visit Rome. Probably during his third missionary journey, on the way back to Jerusalem with the collection he'd received for the poverty-stricken believers there, Paul wrote to the church in Rome anticipating his visit. Because this church has never been visited by an apostle, Paul is at pains to convey the basic truths of the gospel. He presents God's plan of salvation almost like a theological essay. To this mixed congregation he presents God's redemption plan for both Jews and Gentiles, and explains that it is a reason for great joy.

Galatians

No warm greetings open this letter. Paul is astonished that believers are turning to a 'different gospel' (1:6). Some Jewish Christians are proposing that Old Testament ceremonial laws are still binding on believers. Paul strenuously denies this, and reminds them of the true gospel. We are justified by grace through faith in Christ, and this sets the pattern for our Christian lives. We can't earn God's favour by good works. Rather, we grow in Christlikeness by obedience as we live by faith in Christ and rely on the Holy Spirit's power. Joy is just one example of the Spirit's work in our lives.

Day 17

Read Romans 5:1–11
Key verses: Romans 5:1–4

....

Therefore, since we have been justified through faith, we have peace with God through our Lord Jesus Christ, ²through whom we have gained access by faith into this grace in which we now stand. And we boast in the hope of the glory of God. ³Not only so, but we also glory in our sufferings, because we know that suffering produces perseverance; ⁴perseverance, character; and character, hope.

Pure joy? Really? You may think you have little to rejoice about, but Paul urges you to do the following.

• Rejoice in what God has done for you

You are justified. All the sin God held against you has been transferred to Jesus' account, and the sum total of the righteousness of the Lord Jesus has been transferred to your account. You have peace with God and are now standing in grace. God's unmerited favour is enveloping you, at any given moment, under any given set of circumstances.

• Rejoice in your future prospects

'We rejoice in hope of the glory of God' (verse 2, ESV). New Testament hope is overwhelming confidence. We can rejoice because we are totally confident that God will establish a new heaven and a new earth, and we will be with him for ever.

• Rejoice in your present problems

We are not to ignore difficulties, but 'rejoice' (ESV) in them because of what they do (verses 3–5). *Suffering produces perseverance.* It is one thing to trust in Christ when everything is going great. It is entirely different to trust him when things are difficult. *Perseverance produces character.* The word means the evidence of being approved or tested. As we trust in Christ under pressure, the stamp of his approval appears in our lives. *Character produces hope* or confidence. You came through one testing time and found God faithful. There is evidence of his power at work in a new way in your life, so you go into the next testing with an entirely different mindset.

When you know all this, your attitude to pressure changes dramatically. You know what God is allowing and why he is doing it. And all the time, the Holy Spirit is shedding the love of God in your heart (verse 5). He is saying to you, 'I love you so much that I want you to have a little more pressure, so that I can drive you deeper into Christ, so that you can grow up and reflect his glory.' This is how Christians get round to saying, 'I accept it. I don't understand it. I don't appreciate it. But I will rejoice in you in it, because I trust in you and what you are going to accomplish through it.'

• Rejoice in God

So often, we rejoice in God's blessings, but Paul urges us to rejoice in God himself (verse 11, ESV). He repeats this exhortation in Philippians 4:4: 'Rejoice in the Lord always. I will say it again: rejoice!'

Today, practise cultivating joy by rejoicing in one of these – what God has done for you, your future prospects, your present problems, God himself.

Bring joy to your servant, Lord, for I put my trust in you.
(Psalm 86:4)

Day 18

Read Galatians 5:16–26
Key verses: Galatians 5:22–23

....

But the fruit of the Spirit is love, joy, peace, forbear-ance, kindness, goodness, faithfulness, [23]gentleness and self-control. Against such things there is no law.

Imagine bringing a newborn baby back from hospital. Her presence will soon affect your lifestyle and your home. You can no longer do as you choose. A nursery has to be decorated, and sleepless nights will be the norm. But you also witness the miracle, and know the joy of seeing a life develop.

In the same way, when the Holy Spirit resides within you, unless he is neglected or confined to a tiny part of your life, the signs of his presence will soon be evident. He will produce his fruit in your life. This fruit is not something we can manufacture, and it takes time to grow. Sometimes, it involves painful pruning. So don't be discouraged if you haven't produced that perfect supermarket-quality fruit in your life yet. Don't give up. Allow the master gardener, the master pruner, to do his work (John 15:1–17).

Joy is one of the fruits of the Spirit. And this is not enforced jollity or superficial cheerfulness that is liable to change with the weather, but that uncontrived expression of deep trust in God who gives rise to thankfulness and the delight that comes from knowing God is in charge and can be trusted.

It expresses itself in all sorts of ways. Some of us are more extrovert than others, so don't measure the genuineness of someone's joy by whether or not they dance, or swing from the chandeliers! Emotions are not always best judged by outward expression.

This remarkable basket of fruit is composed of nine different kinds, but they all belong together. The picture is rather like one of those blended fruit juice drinks where you can detect the peach, mango, apple and pear that go to make up one rich harmonious mixture. Except this is not extracted juice, but the real fruit. The image is of a fruit basket where all the fruit needs to be displayed. It's not a box of chocolates where you can select your favourite and leave the rest for others to eat. We cannot specialize in joy and so excuse our lack of patience. We may naturally tend towards some fruit rather than others, but we need to let the Spirit cultivate those areas where we are weakest.

What a wonderful picture of a Christlike character this gives!

Do you want to be more joyful, more patient, more self-controlled? These Christlike character qualities can't be manufactured, but a significant element of our present experience of the Spirit is dependent on the next verse in this passage: 'Those who belong to Christ Jesus have crucified the flesh with its passions and desires' (Galatians 5:24). When we became Christians, we were crucified with Christ – our old self (our pre-converted way of life) died, and Christ's death freed us from slavery to sin (Romans 6:6–7). That decisive act gives way to a lifelong process of dying daily, renewing our commitment to reject the impulse to live self-centred lives, and obey the Master Gardener.

> Whoever wants to be my disciple must deny themselves and take up their cross daily and follow me.
> (Luke 9:23)

Philippians

'Joy' is a key theme in this letter. Paul is writing to the church in the Roman colony of Philippi to thank them for their financial gift and update them on his work. He writes about a wide range of issues related to Christian living. He exhorts them to live in humility and unity; warns them against legalists and libertines; and encourages them to stand firm in the face of persecution. However, laced throughout this letter, there is an emphasis on joy – joy in praying, giving, salvation, and culminating (in 4:4) in the call to 'rejoice in the Lord'.

Day 19

Read Philippians 1:1–11
Key verses: Philippians 1:3–4

....

*I thank my God every time I remember you. ⁴In all my
prayers for all of you, I always pray with joy.*

My kids used to groan when I asked them to write 'thank-
you' letters at Christmas. Here Paul is writing a thank-you
letter, but he's not groaning. Rather, he is full of joy. His
joy is even more remarkable when you recall that he is
actually in prison.

In Rome, he is chained to the prison guard and writing to
the Philippian church. This church – of all the churches –
had been most faithful and supportive of his ministry.
When Paul responded to the call to go to Macedonia
during his second missionary journey, he landed in Philippi.

Philippi was significant because it was the first city in
Europe that Paul evangelized. His first convert was Lydia.
Then he ran into trouble when he cast out an evil spirit

from a slave girl. He was arrested, beaten and thrown into prison. He was singing praises at midnight when an earthquake shook the building and, in the aftermath, the jailer was amazingly converted (Acts 16:25–34).

In prison, Paul couldn't do anything for these new converts except pray. His prayer life is marked by thanksgiving and joy: 'I thank my God every time I remember you. In all my prayers for all of you, I always pray with joy.'

Like most people, I struggle with prayer. One of the things that I've discovered is that if I begin my prayers with rejoicing in the Lord, intercession then becomes easier. So begin your prayers with praise and thanksgiving, by reflecting on what God has done for you and rejoicing in his mercy.

The letter to the Philippians is all about joy. Sixteen times Paul mentions joy, and Philippians 1:4 is the first of those. Joy is to be an essential characteristic of the Christian's life. Paul writes in Galatians 5:22–23, 'The fruit of the Spirit is love, joy, peace, forbearance, kindness, goodness, faithfulness, gentleness and self-control' (see Day 18). Paul is saying that that fruit characterizes every Christian. Joy is not a matter of temperament, circumstances or mood. Our joy is in the Lord; we rejoice in God's goodness. And so Paul is in prison, he's facing an uncertain future, but he is full of joy.

Today, start your prayers by rejoicing in God.

O blessed Jesus, Your love is wonderful! It is the admiration, joy and song of glorified saints . . . It was love which moved You to . . . become obedient unto death, even the death of the cross! . . . You sought and found me when I sought You not. You spoke peace to me in the day of my distress, when the clouds of guilt and darkness hung heavy on my soul . . . You have borne with all my weakness, corrected my mistakes, restored me from my wanderings, and healed my backslidings. May Your lovingkindness be ever before my eyes to induce me to walk in Your truth. May Your love be the daily theme of my meditations, and the constant joy of my heart!

(John Fawcett, *Christ Precious to Those Who Believe*, Bottom of the Hill Publishing, 2013)

Day 20

Read Philippians 1:1–11
Key verses: Philippians 1:4–6

....

In all my prayers for all of you, I always pray with joy *5because of your partnership in the gospel from the first day until now, 6being confident of this, that he who began a good work in you will carry it on to completion until the day of Christ Jesus.*

What is Paul joyful about?

As he sits in his prison cell praying, he is praising God 'because of your partnership [your fellowship, Greek *koinonia*] in the gospel from the first day until now' (verse 5). Paul is thrilled as he reflects on his fellowship with the Philippians. From the very beginning, the moment that God began a work in Philippi, the believers began to care for him. The first convert was Lydia (see Day 19). The Lord opened her heart, and what did she do? She opened her home (Acts 16:13–15). The Lord opened the heart of the Philippian jailer, and what did do? He opened his home

(Acts 16:34). Even after Paul left Philippi, this church continued to care for him. The Christians prayed for him and sent financial support. Indeed, part of the reason he writes this letter is to thank them for their generosity and faithfulness (Philippians 4:10–20). Paul even mentions the sacrifice of these believers when he's writing to the Corinthians:

> And now, brothers and sisters, we want you to know about the grace that God has given the Macedonian churches. In the midst of a very severe trial, their overflowing joy and their extreme poverty welled up in rich generosity. For I testify that they gave as much as they were able, and even beyond their ability.
> (2 Corinthians 8:1–3)

The Philippians gave in great joy, despite their poverty. They gave more than they could afford to give because they loved Paul so much. The believers stood shoulder to shoulder with Paul, and it brought him tremendous joy. It is still a blessing to the Lord's people and to the ministry of the Lord's people when we give.

We often wrestle with giving. We worry whether we will have enough money left over and whether our sacrifice is actually worth it. But financial giving is part of our discipleship, and our bank statements are a reflection of what is most precious to us. God himself is a lavish giver – he sent his beloved Son to die for us – and we mirror his character when we cheerfully give generously to his people.

Who is thanking God today for you and your partnership in the gospel? To whom are you bringing joy because of your prayers, love and financial support? Don't miss out on the joy – give yourself and your resources to God's people and his work.

> I know, dear God, that you care nothing for the surface – you want *us*, our true selves – and so I have given from the heart, honestly and happily. And now see all these people doing the same, giving freely, willingly – what a joy! O GOD, God of our fathers Abraham, Isaac, and Israel, keep this generous spirit alive for ever in these people always, keep their hearts set firmly in you.
> (1 Chronicles 29:14–19, MSG)

Day 21

Read Philippians 1:1–11
Key verses: Philippians 1:4–6

....

*In all my prayers for all of you, I always pray with joy
⁵because of your partnership in the gospel from the
first day until now, ⁶being confident of this, that he
who began a good work in you will carry it on to
completion until the day of Christ Jesus.*

There is something bigger, more profound, that causes
Paul's joy.

Yes, he is delighted by the Philippians' financial support,
but he is much more thrilled that they have been saved
by God. Look at verse 6: who is the author of the work?
It is God.

The underlying, constant theme of the Bible is that salvation is of the Lord. God is the one who planned, and
who executes and applies salvation. When I was converted
at the age of eleven, I thought that I had come to God,

that's what it felt like. But as I look back and reflect, I know it was God who drew me to himself. The Bible sometimes speaks of salvation as a work of God *for* you (you are justified); it also speaks of a work of God *in* you (you are sanctified, transformed into the likeness of God).

The phrase 'work of God' is from the Greek word that can be used of creation. Just as God created the universe, God creates something in our lives. One of my friends put it like this: 'God created the universe by preaching a sermon.' It's true, isn't it? He spoke, and the words of God had such power that the universe came into existence. In the same way, God began to create a new work in your life by a sermon, by his Word and his Spirit together. This good work within us will be brought to completion on the day of Jesus Christ.

Philippians 3:20 describes the ultimate outcome of salvation: 'Our citizenship is in heaven. And we eagerly await a Saviour from there, the Lord Jesus Christ, who, by the power that enables him to bring everything under his control, will transform our lowly bodies so that they will be like his glorious body.' The completion of God's work will be a brand new, transformed, spiritual body like the body of Christ. It will not just be an immortal body, bereft of aches and pains, but it will be a perfect body, unable to sin. God will finish what he started; his work is from conversion to consummation.

So Paul, in his prison cell, is able to rejoice that he can leave these Philippian believers in the hands of God.

Today, praise God for evidence of his transforming power in the lives of those around you. Rejoice in his promise to complete the work in their lives and yours.

> If we are saved by grace alone, this salvation is a constant source of amazed delight. Nothing is mundane or matter-of-fact about our lives. It is a miracle we are Christians, and the gospel, which creates bold humility, should give us a far deeper sense of humour and joy. We don't take ourselves seriously, and we are full of hope for the world.
>
> (Tim Keller, *Loving the City: Doing Balanced, Gospel-Centered Ministry in Your City*, Zondervan, 2016, pp. 50–51)

James and 1 Peter

'Joy in suffering' is a repeated theme in the letters written by James, Jesus' brother, and Peter the apostle. Both explain that joy in dark days is possible, not because we take pleasure in pain, but because we value what God is achieving through our suffering. God is growing our Christian character, deepening our faith and bringing glory to Christ – and this is worth rejoicing in.

James

Stephen's martyrdom in Jerusalem signalled a mass exodus, as believers fled throughout the Roman Empire. As leader of the Jerusalem church, what words of encouragement would James write to these persecuted believers? Perhaps a little surprisingly, his key message was: faith works. Genuine belief inevitably transforms our speech, suffering, priorities and every other aspect of life. In just five chapters, James briefly touches upon a whole variety of issues that concern these new believers. He doesn't give an exhaustive treatise on any one topic, but simply urges them to live out their faith, knowing that there is a value and purpose to their suffering.

1 Peter

The believers scattered through Asia Minor (modern-day Turkey) were not prepared for the persecution they were facing. So Peter reminded them of God's eternal purposes. He urged them to rejoice in the hope of their inheritance, knowing that suffering was only temporary, and paled in comparison to the eternal glory they would enjoy. He also encouraged them with the example of Jesus' suffering and the privilege of belonging to God's people. The purpose of his letter was to give these pilgrims confidence in God's grace, whatever circumstances they faced: 'I have written to you briefly, encouraging you and testifying that this is the true grace of God. Stand fast in it' (1 Peter 5:12).

Day 22

Read James 1:1–8
Key verses: James 1:2–3

....

Consider it pure joy, my brothers and sisters, whenever you face trials of many kinds, [3]because you know that the testing of your faith produces perseverance.

Pure joy? Really?

James is advocating something completely counter-intuitive. Nothing stuns the unbeliever more than seeing a Christian able to be joyful in the midst of suffering. It is not a matter of 'Hallelujah anyway', but it is a joy very deep within, present regardless of the circumstances.

There wasn't a lot of joy in the Jewish tradition. Elements came through in the Old Testament, like Habakkuk's declaration: 'Though the fig-tree does not bud . . . and the fields produce no food . . . yet I will rejoice in the LORD, I will be joyful in God my Saviour' (Habakkuk 3:17–18; see Day 12). And when we come to the New Testament, we find James challenging us in the same way as his brother, his Lord, did. In John 16:22, for example, when Jesus says, 'No one will take away your joy', the context is suffering. Jesus' point was that those who oppose you may hurt you, they may persecute you, they may kill you, but no one can take away your joy. And so, in the context of suffering, Jesus is able to promise, 'Ask . . . and your joy will be complete' (John 16:24; see Day 15).

This joy is an anchor for our soul. Remember Luke 10, where the seventy-two had been sent out on mission and came back overwhelmed with all that had happened: 'They . . . returned with joy and said, "Lord, even the demons submit to us in your name"' (verse 17). But Jesus' response is significant: 'Do not rejoice that the spirits submit to you, but rejoice that your names are written in heaven' (verse 20). If your success or failure is dependent on circumstances – how well your ministry is doing, how well your children are behaving, how robust your finances are – you are going to be on a rollercoaster, forever tossed about by your feelings. But if you are focused on the thing that can never change, your name being written in heaven, your joy will be full, all the time, even in the midst of suffering.

This joy also gives tremendous assurance. Jesus said, 'Blessed are you when people insult you, persecute you and falsely say all kinds of evil against you because of me. Rejoice and be glad, because great is your reward in heaven' (Matthew 5:11–12). Amid the harsh realities and overwhelming uncertainties of life, we can be joyful because the Lord knows what we are facing, cares about us and will reward our faithfulness.

Joy in God in the midst of suffering makes the worth of God – the all-satisfying glory of God – shine more brightly than it would through our joy at any other time. Sunshine happiness signals the value of sunshine. But happiness in suffering signals the value of God. Suffering and hardship joyfully accepted in the path of obedience to Christ show the supremacy of Christ more than all our faithfulness in fair days.

(John Piper, in *Feed My Sheep*, Evangelical Press, 2009, p. 139)

Day 23

Read James 1:1–8
Key verses: James 1:2–3

....

Consider it pure joy, my brothers and sisters, whenever you face trials of many kinds, ³because you know that the testing of your faith produces perseverance.

When tragedy strikes or when suffering comes, it is often difficult to summon up joy. That is why it is startling that James starts his letter with the words: 'Consider it pure joy . . . whenever you face trials.' The sentiment is, 'Consider it nothing but joy'. To 'consider' implies a settled conviction. In a sense, you need that conviction before the problems strike. It means you have thought about suffering, you have looked at what the Bible teaches, and you have decided that when difficulties arise, whatever life throws at you, you are going to trust the Lord.

In part, this conviction comes because 'you know' the value of these trials (verse 3). You are convinced they have a benefit. James says the trials you face – of various kinds – will result in perseverance. We can have deep-seated joy even in trials because we know that they are growing our Christian character. Peter has a similar message: 'In all this [i.e. the suffering] you greatly rejoice, though now for a little while you may have had to suffer grief in all kinds of trials.' Why? 'These have come so that the proven genuineness of your faith – of greater worth than gold, which perishes even though refined by fire – may result in praise, glory and honour when Jesus Christ is revealed' (1 Peter 1:6–7; see Days 24–26).

Do you have this settled conviction that James talks about? Are you ready to 'consider it pure joy' when trials come? Will you follow the example of the Apostle Paul: 'sorrowful, yet always rejoicing' (2 Corinthians 6:10)? The writer to the Hebrews urges believers – then and now – to hold fast to this conviction:

> Remember those earlier days after you had received the light, when you endured in a great conflict full of suffering. Sometimes you were publicly exposed to insult and per-secution; at other times you stood side by side with those who were so treated. You suffered along with those in prison and joyfully accepted the confiscation of your property, because you knew that you yourselves had better

and lasting possessions. So do not throw away your confidence; it will be richly rewarded.
(Hebrews 10:32–35)

We can be joyful, even in suffering, because we know God is working out his purposes in us; he is making us more like Jesus. And as we become more like the Christ and press on in obedience, there is even more joy!

Jesus said, 'If you obey My commands, you will remain in My love, just as I have obeyed My Father's commands and remain in His love. I have told you this so that My joy may be in you and that your joy may be complete' (Jn. 15:10–11). In this statement, Jesus links obedience and joy in a cause and effect manner; that is, joy results from obedience. Only those who are obedient – who are pursuing holiness as a way of life – will know the joy that comes from God.
(Jerry Bridges, *The Pursuit of Holiness*, NavPress, 2016, p. 123)

Day 24

Read 1 Peter 1:1–12
Key verses: 1 Peter 1:3–6

....

Praise be to the God and Father of our Lord Jesus Christ! In his great mercy he has given us new birth into a living hope through the resurrection of Jesus Christ from the dead, ⁴and into an inheritance that can never perish, spoil or fade. This inheritance is kept in heaven for you, ⁵who through faith are shielded by God's power until the coming of the salvation that is ready to be revealed in the last time. ⁶In all this you greatly rejoice, though now for a little while you may have had to suffer grief in all kinds of trials.

We might like to imagine that the hopeful person is the optimist, who lives above the hassles of this world in the perennial pleasure of watching things get better. But in these verses, Peter places hope – our certain hope of Jesus' return, our resurrected bodies like his, our inheritance kept in heaven for us and us for it – in the context of suffering. He says we have only been introduced to hope; we are now receiving the goal of our faith, the salvation of our souls, yet we have not seen Jesus Christ and we still live with trials and opposition. In these verses, Peter provides several reasons why, while we may have to suffer, Christians actually rejoice in this hope.

The first reason is intrinsic. The suffering is temporary: it is transient. 'Though now for a little while you may have had to suffer grief in all kinds of trials', over against the fruitfulness and inheritance of an eternity with God. Small wonder then that, in 2 Corinthians 4, after many brutal experiences imposed both by the world and by churches that had gone astray, Paul can speak of his light and momentary afflictions, which cannot be compared with the eternal weight of glory:

> Therefore we do not lose heart. Though outwardly we are wasting away, yet inwardly we are being renewed day by day. For our light and momentary troubles are achieving for us an eternal glory that far outweighs them all. So we fix our eyes not on what is seen, but on what is unseen, since what is seen is temporary, but what is unseen is eternal.
> (2 Corinthians 4:16–18)

This is not how I'm inclined to see things when I am suffering. My entire horizon can be consumed by some small aggravation. Anyone who has ever served in church for any period of time knows full well that sooner or later you get kicked in the teeth, and then it is difficult to imagine any reward compensating for it. But that's not the way Peter saw it. No, the 'light and momentary troubles' Paul writes of, and this 'little while' Peter writes of, cannot be compared with the eternal weight of glory.

Don't let suffering extinguish your joy. Imagine your grief as simply a drop in the bucket compared to the ocean of eternal glory that is waiting for you. Today, determine to rejoice in the hope of your eternal inheritance.

May the God of hope fill you with all joy and peace in believing, so that by the power of the Holy Spirit, you may abound in hope.
(Romans 15:13, ESV)

Day 25

Read 1 Peter 1:1–12
Key verses: 1 Peter 1:6–7

....

In all this you greatly rejoice, though now for a little while you may have had to suffer grief in all kinds of trials. ⁷ These have come so that the proven genuineness of your faith – of greater worth than gold, which perishes even though refined by fire – may result in praise, glory and honour when Jesus Christ is revealed.

Imagine if you had a really rough time before you became a Christian, but afterwards everything was smooth sailing. Would that increase your faith, in this broken, self-centred world? No, not at all! In these verses, Peter gives another reason why we can rejoice in trials. He explains that the tension between present pressures and the ultimate glory to come is precisely what strengthens our faith and produces endurance. It demonstrates that our faith is genuine, and it deepens that faith (verse 7).

This is a fairly common theme in New Testament writings. For example, 'Consider it pure joy, my brothers and sisters, whenever you face trials of many kinds' (James 1:2). That doesn't mean we are masochists. It tells us we should rejoice: 'because you know that the testing of your faith produces perseverance. Let perseverance finish its work so that you may be mature and complete, not lacking anything' (James 1:3–4; see Days 22 and 23). With God in charge, what this is really designed to do is to make us become enduring. Just as the endurance that an athlete pushes himself towards will produce endurance characteristic of his very being, so also with trials on the Christian way. And Christians prize endurance becoming part of our very being, just as an athlete does.

But it is not just strengthening in maturity and endurance in this life. There is something more: 'Blessed is the one who perseveres under trial because, having stood the test, that person will receive the crown of life that the Lord has promised to those who love him' (James 1:12). In other words, Christians do not have the same sort of values as the secular world that knows nothing of the rewards of heaven. We can look at trials in a different way, we can rejoice in them, precisely because we have this Christian hope.

Paul and James both say that we should rejoice in our trials because of their beneficial results. It is not the adversity considered in itself that is to be the ground of our joy. Rather, it is the expectation of the results, the development of our character, that should cause us to rejoice in adversity. God does not ask us to rejoice because we have lost our job, or a loved one has been stricken with cancer, or a child has been born with an incurable birth defect. But He does tell us to rejoice because we believe He is in control of those circumstances and is at work through them for our ultimate good.

(Jerry Bridges, *Trusting God*, NavPress, 2017, p. 175)

Day 26

Read 1 Peter 1:1–12
Key verses: 1 Peter 1:7–9

. . . .

These [trials] have come so that the proven genuineness of your faith – of greater worth than gold, which perishes even though refined by fire – may result in praise, glory and honour when Jesus Christ is revealed. ⁸Though you have not seen him, you love him; and even though you do not see him now, you believe in him and are filled with an inexpressible and glorious joy, ⁹for you are receiving the end result of your faith, the salvation of your souls.

Why rejoice in suffering? In this passage, Peter gives one further reason: the rewards are spectacular and actually begin now.

According to verse 7, our faith is proved genuine under trial and results in praise, glory and honour when Jesus Christ is revealed. Is this praise, glory and honour for us or for God? Commentators are divided over this, and you can make sense of the text either way. In his writings, Peter constantly says that the ultimate praise goes to God or Jesus (1 Peter 2:9; 4:11). Yet he also says we will receive a crown of glory at the end (1 Peter 5:4). Of course, our glory and Christ's glory are bound together. Any glory we ultimately receive is still a sharing of Christ's glory. So the thought of all praise being directed to God at the end is essential to this passage. And now, Christians already delight to see whatever praise and honour and glory come to God through Jesus Christ, even in our sufferings.

There will certainly be joy at Christ's second coming, but we can also rejoice now because the rewards start now. Christians are related to Jesus already, hence verses 8–9. Peter had seen Jesus, but he writes to people like us who have never seen him, yet who, by faith, love him. We are in a relationship with Jesus; we have been saved by him; the new birth has been given to us; the Holy Spirit has come upon us because of all God's design work in sending Jesus to sprinkle his blood on us and clean us up. We do not see him now, but we believe in him, and we are filled with an inexpressible and glorious joy. Why? We are receiving the goal of our faith, the salvation of our souls.

When asked what the rewards for Christians were, the fourth-century church father Gregory of Nyssa (c.335–c.395) answered,

It seems to me that for which we hope is nothing other than the Lord himself.

For He himself is the judge of those who contend, and the crown for those who win.

He is the one who distributes the inheritance, he himself is the good inheritance.

He is the good portion and the giver of the portion; he is the one who makes riches and is himself the riches.

He shows you the treasure, and is himself your treasure.

(Gregory of Nyssa, *The Beatitudes*, Homily 8)

Day 27

Read 1 Peter 4:12–19
Key verses: 1 Peter 4:12–13

∙∙∙

Dear friends, do not be surprised at the fiery ordeal that has come on you to test you, as though something strange were happening to you. ¹³But rejoice inasmuch as you participate in the sufferings of Christ, so that you may be overjoyed when his glory is revealed.

Imagine you did a small painting and suddenly, to your surprise, you found it on exhibition in London alongside great masters like Rembrandt and Van Gogh. You wouldn't say, 'Didn't I add to that occasion!' You would probably say, 'Why did they choose my work to put up there?' But you would certainly look at your painting in a different way from then on.

Similarly, we don't add anything to the sufferings of Christ, but when we suffer, we are privileged to have our suffering placed at the same level as his. Peter is saying, 'When you suffer, make no mistake; your suffering goes into the same hall of fame as the suffering of Jesus. So don't just put up with it – rejoice in it!' This is hard to do, but I have come to believe that it is possible to rejoice with tears in your eyes; when your heart is broken; when you actually feel so numb you wonder whether you will ever feel again – because you know that it is going to be all right, because, in God's hands, it *is* all right.

You can rejoice through the tears and pain, and that is precisely what Peter is commending here, 'so that you may be overjoyed when his glory is revealed'. You see, Christians are in effect putting all their eggs in one basket. They are saying, 'If the gospel message isn't true, I'm sunk.' But the other side of that is, when it is proved to be true, we'll be overjoyed.

Every bit of suffering is leading to the day when we'll join in the glad song of praise, to the glory of the Lord. We rejoice now, but on that great glory-day, when Jesus Christ is unveiled, we will be overjoyed. With this in mind, keep telling people the good news of the gospel so that they too can share in this joy.

Today, lift your eyes from your present troubles and focus on the future. Consider your suffering and gospel witness in the light of that great glory-day when you will be overjoyed in the presence of Christ.

If there lurks in most modern minds the notion that to desire our own good and earnestly hope for the enjoyment of it is a bad thing, I submit that this notion has crept in from Kant and the Stoics and is no part of the Christian faith. Indeed, if we consider the unblushing promises of reward and the staggering nature of the rewards promised in the Gospels, it would seem that Our Lord finds our desires not too strong, but too weak. We are half-hearted creatures, fooling around with drink and sex and ambition when infinite joy is offered us, like an ignorant child who wants to go on making mud pies in the slum because he cannot imagine what is meant by the offer of a holiday at the sea. We are far too easily pleased.
(C. S. Lewis, *The Weight of Glory*, William Collins, 2013, p. 26)

1 John

In his later years, John, Jesus' beloved disciple, was pastor of the church at Ephesus. It seems that this letter was probably a circular written to the other churches in the province of Asia. John was primarily writing to combat Gnosticism. This heresy taught that the spirit was entirely good and matter, the body, was entirely bad. The teaching had three main consequences – Jesus' humanity was denied; salvation was believed to be an escape from the body and the acquisition of special knowledge rather than having faith in Christ; and lack of morality was rife because it didn't matter what you did with your body. John wrote as an eyewitness to testify to the incarnation of Christ and to assure the believers of their salvation. He wanted the Christians to know that they could base their whole lives on the truths of the gospel, and that this was the source of true joy.

Day 28

Read 1 John 1:1–10
Key verses: 1 John 1:1–2

....

That which was from the beginning, which we have heard, which we have seen with our eyes, which we have looked at and our hands have touched – this we proclaim concerning the Word of life. ²The life appeared; we have seen it and testify to it, and we proclaim to you the eternal life, which was with the Father and has appeared to us.

Is your joy complete?

John writes this letter 'to make our joy complete' (verse 4). He's not merely talking about fullness of joy here and now. He's looking forward to all that will be ours in the future too, since 'in your presence is fullness of joy; at your right hand are pleasures forevermore' (Psalm 16:11, NKJV). Such joy mirrors something at the very heart of deity, the mutual delight that the triune God has in himself. This 'joy of the Lord' in turn becomes 'our strength'

(Nehemiah 8:10; see Day 1). While happiness depends on happenings, God's joy depends on Jesus!

There can be no real joy if what Christians believe is not true. John wants believers to know, beyond a shadow of a doubt, that they are loved by their Father, redeemed by his Son, indwelt by his Spirit, and headed for eternal life. So he carefully sets out how the gospel is based on apostolic, eyewitness testimony. He testifies that 'we have *heard* . . . we have *seen* with our eyes . . . we have *looked at*'. Then, amazingly, he adds, 'our *hands have touched*'. This echoes the scene in which the resurrected Christ appeared to the apostles and said, 'Touch me and see; a ghost does not have flesh and bones, as you see I have' (Luke 24:39). This apostle had taken a long, hard look at the risen Christ, and elsewhere affirmed: 'we *beheld* his glory' (John 1:14, KJV).

Notice the interplay in these verses between 'we' and 'you'. You and I are not eyewitnesses of the risen Christ. We were not there in the first century. But, thank God, we rely on the testimony of the men and women who were.

We do well to remember that the Christian faith's credibility has been contested from its earliest days. Today, we are Christians because 'we did not follow cleverly devised stories' (2 Peter 1:16). There are good, rock-solid, reasons why we have the writings that make up our New Testament. These documents have apostolic authority, as John, for example, reminds us here: 'The life appeared; we have seen it and testify to it, and we proclaim to you the eternal life' (1 John 1:2). Here is a first-century eye-witness testifying to who Jesus Christ is, and what he has done. We'll never have joy if we think the whole Christian story might just be a tissue of lies. Our joy is grounded in knowing that the gospel is true, resting as it does on apostolic authority.

Eternity has invaded time; the eternal has become one of us! This is a truth to rejoice in.

The happy life is joy based on truth. This is joy grounded in you, O God, who are the truth.
(Augustine, *The Confessions*, ed. Henry Chadwick, OUP, 2008, p. 199)

Day 29

Read 1 John 1:5–10
Key verses: 1 John 1:5–6

....

This is the message we have heard from him and declare to you: God is light; in him there is no darkness at all. ⁶If we claim to have fellowship with him and yet walk in the darkness, we lie and do not live out the truth.

Our joy can be extinguished when we are confronted with God's holiness and purity. How could we approach a God like this? How could we ever stand before One who is described as 'a consuming fire' (Hebrews 12:29)?

One option, found in these verses, is to deny the problem of human sinfulness. People don't like the word 'sin', or to admit their own sinfulness. Notice here three 'if we claim' statements (verses 6, 8 and 10). Verse 6 highlights how sin can lead us into self-deception: 'If we claim to have fellowship with him and yet walk in the darkness, we lie and do not live out the truth.' Verse 8 is a flat denial that sin exists in our nature: 'If we claim to be without sin, we deceive ourselves and the truth is not in us.' 'Sin' here is in its singular form, indicating that this is our human condition; we have sinful natures before we commit sins in particular. Finally, in verse 10, there is a denial of our sinful actions: 'If we claim we have not sinned, we make him out to be a liar and his Word is not in us.'

How do we make God a liar? Well, God's Word consistently affirms: 'There is no one who does not sin' (1 Kings 8:46); 'All have sinned and fall short of the glory of God' (Romans 3:23). We are all part of a broken, fallen, sinful race. We sin and we are sinned against. If we insist on our own righteousness and goodness, then we'll never need Jesus Christ who came to seek and to save that which was lost (Luke 19:10). But without Jesus, we'll never know the joy of eternity invading our hearts. In effect, we're saying: 'Maybe Jesus' death was for really bad people or folks who are a bit unhinged, but it isn't for nice, law-abiding people like me.' In doing so, we make God a liar, because he tells us we are all sinners in his holy sight. No one likes to be told they're in the wrong, but that's the truth about us all before a holy God. But when we own our sinfulness, trusting that Christ's death on the cross has paid the penalty for our sin, then we can come into God's presence with confidence, with joyful and thankful hearts.

Light and darkness cannot coexist. Today, ask God to shine his light on your life and expose sins that need his forgiveness – secret sins, unknown sins, habitual sins: 'Search me, God, and know my heart . . . See if there is any offensive way in me' (Psalm 139:23–24). Then, with joy and gratitude, live consciously in God's holy presence.

> Blessed are those who have learned to acclaim you,
>   who walk in the light of your presence, LORD.
> They rejoice in your name all day long;
>   they celebrate your righteousness.
> (Psalm 89:15–16)

Day 30

Read 1 John 1:5 – 2:2
Key verses: 1 John 1:7, 9

....

But if we walk in the light, as he is in the light, we have fellowship with one another, and the blood of Jesus, his Son, purifies us from all sin . . . ⁹If we confess our sins, he is faithful and just and will forgive us our sins and purify us from all unrighteousness.

Guilt is a major thief of joy. Many people are consumed by it for sins that may have haunted them for five, twenty-five, forty-five years, and even more. But the gospel tells us that in the violent, sacrificial, atoning death of Jesus – that's what 'blood' means in verse 7 – we can be cleansed from sin and guilt.

What a promise verse 9 contains: 'If we confess our sins, he is faithful and just and will forgive us our sins'. The word translated 'confess' is literally to 'say the same', 'agree'. When we confess our sins, we're simply agreeing with God who knew all about our sins anyway! But our sins can only be covered if we will uncover them to God: 'Whoever conceals their sins does not prosper, but the one who confesses and renounces them finds mercy' (Proverbs 28:13). As we confess our sins, God is faithful to his promise to forgive. On what basis? All is based on the ultimate sacrifice, the death of Jesus Christ, his eternal Son, in our place, to bring a rebel people home to God for ever.

Christians are wise to remember three things about sin: don't 'expect', excuse or excite it. John, with a pastor's heart, reminds us, 'if anybody does sin, we have an advocate with the Father – Jesus Christ, the Righteous One' (1 John 2:1). The word 'advocate' is the same one used of the Holy Spirit's ministry (John 14:16). It conveys the idea of having someone alongside you, one who may speak and act in your defence. The astonishing message of the gospel is: we are guilty as charged. However, in heaven's court, our 'defence lawyer' speaks up for us, and he never loses a case.

Jesus is not only our advocate but 'the atoning sacrifice for our sins, and not only for ours but also for the sins of the whole world' (1 John 2:2). He has turned aside the wrath of God. Automatically and for everyone? Not quite! Rather, it is for all who confess their need, relying on the blood of Jesus as sufficient to cleanse from every sin.

Do we want 'our joy complete' (1 John 1:4)? Then accept his gift of forgiveness, relying alone on Christ. Then in his sight, we are clean and whole again. Hallelujah!

Jesus has died in our place, satisfied God's wrath, and is now interceding for us before his Father. We are forgiven, so let's not hold on to our guilt a moment longer. Take God at his word when he says he will 'cleanse us from all sin'. Pray with King David, 'Restore to me the joy of your salvation, and make me willing to obey you' (Psalm 51:12, NLT).

> When Satan tempts me to despair and tells me
>   of the guilt within,
> Upward I look and see him there, who made
>   an end of all my sin!
> Because the sinless Saviour died, my sinful soul
>   is counted free
> For God the just is satisfied to look on him and
>   pardon me.
> (Charitie Lees Bancroft, 'Before the Throne of God Above', 1863)

For further study

If you would like to read more on the theme of joy, you might find the following selection of books helpful.

- Tim Chester, *Enjoying God* (Good Book Company, 2018).

- Tim Keller, *The Freedom of Self-forgetfulness: The Path to Christian Joy* (10Publishing, 2012).

- Paul Mallard, *Staying Fresh: Serving with Joy* (IVP, 2015).

- John Piper, *When I Don't Desire God: How to Fight for Joy* (Crossway, 2013).

- Mike Reeves, *The Good God: Enjoying Father, Son and Spirit* (Paternoster, 2013).

- Helen Roseveare, *Count It All Joy* (Christian Focus, 2017).

Bible and other acknowledgments

Unless otherwise noted, Scripture quotations are taken from The Holy Bible, New International Version (Anglicized edition). Copyright © 1979, 1984, 2011 by Biblica. Used by permission of Hodder & Stoughton Ltd, an Hachette UK company. All rights reserved.'NIV' is a registered trademark of Biblica. UK trademark number 1448790.

Quotations marked ESV are taken from the ESV Bible (The Holy Bible, English Standard Version), copyright © 2001 by Crossway, a publishing ministry of Good News Publishers. Used by permission. All rights reserved.

Quotations marked KJV are taken from the Authorized Version of the Bible (The King James Bible), the rights in which are vested in the Crown, and are reproduced by permission of the Crown's Patentee, Cambridge University Press.

Quotations marked MSG are taken from *THE MESSAGE*. Copyright © by Eugene H. Peterson 1993, 1994, 1995, 1996, 2000, 2001, 2002. Used by permission of NavPress Publishing Group.

Quotations marked NKJV are taken from the New King James Version. Copyright © 1982 by Thomas Nelson, Inc. Used by permission. All rights reserved.

Quotations marked NLT are taken from the *Holy Bible*, New Living Translation, copyright © 1996. Used by permission of Tyndale House Publishers, Inc., Carol Stream, Illinois 60189, USA. All rights reserved.

Quotation on p. xvi from *Letters to Malcolm: Chiefly on Prayer* by C. S. Lewis © copyright C. S. Lewis Pte Ltd 1963, 1964. Reproduced with permission.

Quotation on p. 98 from *The Weight of Glory* by C. S. Lewis © copyright C. S. Lewis Pte Ltd 1949. Reproduced with permission.

Keswick Ministries

Our purpose

Keswick Ministries exists to inspire and equip Christians to love and live for Christ in his world.

God's purpose is to bring his blessing to all the nations of the world (Genesis 12:3). That promise of blessing, which touches every aspect of human life, is ultimately fulfilled through the life, death, resurrection, ascension and future return of Christ. All of the people of God are called to participate in his missionary purposes, wherever he may place them. The central vision of Keswick Ministries is to see the people of God equipped, inspired and refreshed to fulfil that calling, directed and guided by God's Word in the power of his Spirit, for the glory of his Son.

Our priorities

There are three fundamental priorities which shape all that we do as we look to serve the local church.

- *Hearing God's Word*: the Scriptures are the foundation for the church's life, growth and mission, and Keswick Ministries is committed to preach and teach God's

Word in a way that is faithful to Scripture and relevant to Christians of all ages and backgrounds.

- *Becoming like God's Son*: from its earliest days, the Keswick movement has encouraged Christians to live godly lives in the power of the Spirit, to grow in Christ-likeness and to live under his lordship in every area of life. This is God's will for his people in every culture and generation.

- *Serving God's mission*: the authentic response to God's Word is obedience to his mission, and the inevitable result of Christlikeness is sacrificial service. Keswick Ministries seeks to encourage committed discipleship in family life, work and society, and energetic engagement in the cause of world mission.

Our ministry

- *Keswick Convention.* The Convention attracts some 12,000 to 15,000 Christians from the UK and around the world to Keswick every summer. It provides Bible teaching for all ages, vibrant worship, a sense of unity across generations and denominations, and an inspirational call to serve Christ in the world. It caters for children of all ages and has a strong youth and young adult programme. And it all takes place in the beautiful

Lake District – a perfect setting for rest, recreation and refreshment.

- *Keswick fellowship.* For more than 140 years, the work of Keswick has had an impact on churches worldwide, not just through individuals being changed but also through Bible conventions that originate or draw their inspiration from the Keswick Convention. Today, there is a network of events that shares Keswick Ministries' priorities across the UK and in many parts of Europe, Asia, North America, Australia, Africa and the Caribbean. Keswick Ministries is committed to strengthening the network in the UK and beyond, through prayer, news and cooperative activity.

- *Keswick teaching and training.* Keswick Ministries is developing a range of inspiring, equipping, Bible-centred teaching and training that focuses on 'whole-of-life' discipleship. This builds on the same concern that started the Convention: that all Christians live godly lives in the power of the Spirit in all spheres of life in God's world. Some of the events focus on equipping. They are smaller and more intensive. Others focus on inspiring. Some are for pastors, others for those in other forms of church leadership, while many are for any Christian. All courses aim to see participants return home refreshed to serve.

- *Keswick resources.* Keswick Ministries produces a range of books, devotionals and study guides as well as digital resources to inspire and equip Christians to live for Christ. The printed resources focus on the core foundations of Christian life and mission and help Christians in their walk with Christ. The digital resources make teaching and sung worship from the Keswick Convention available in a variety of ways.

Our unity

The Keswick movement worldwide has adopted a key Pauline statement to describe its gospel inclusivity: 'all one in Christ Jesus' (Galatians 3:28). Keswick Ministries works with evangelicals from a wide variety of church backgrounds, on the understanding that they share a commitment to the essential truths of the Christian faith as set out in our statement of belief.

Our contact details

T: 01768 780075
E: info@keswickministries.org
W: www.keswickministries.org
Mail: Keswick Ministries, Rawnsley Centre, Main Street, Keswick, Cumbria, CA12 5NP, England

Related titles from IVP

Food for the Journey

The Food for the Journey series offers daily devotionals from well-loved
Bible teachers at the Keswick Convention in an ideal pocket-sized format –
to accompany you wherever you go.

Available in the series

1 Thessalonians

Alec Motyer with
Elizabeth McQuoid
978 1 78359 439 9

2 Timothy

Michael Baughen with
Elizabeth McQuoid
978 1 78359 438 2

Colossians

Steve Brady with
Elizabeth McQuoid
978 1 78359 722 2

Ezekiel

Liam Goligher with
Elizabeth McQuoid
978 1 78359 603 4

Habakkuk

Jonathan Lamb with
Elizabeth McQuoid
978 1 78359 652 2

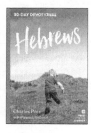

Hebrews

Charles Price with
Elizabeth McQuoid
978 1 78359 611 9

James

Stuart Briscoe with
Elizabeth McQuoid
978 1 78359 523 5

John 14 - 17

Simon Manchester with
Elizabeth McQuoid
978 1 78359 495 5

Available from your local Christian bookshop or **www.ivpbooks.com**

Food for the Journey

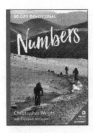   

Numbers
Christopher Wright
with Elizabeth
McQuoid
978 1 78359 720 8

Revelation 1 - 3
Paul Mallard with
Elizabeth McQuoid
978 1 78359 712 3

Romans 5 - 8
John Stott with
Elizabeth McQuoid
978 1 78359 718 5

Ruth
Alistair Begg with
Elizabeth McQuoid
978 1 78359 525 9

Praise for the series

'This devotional series is biblically rich,
theologically deep and full of wisdom . . .
I recommend it highly.' Becky Manley Pippert,
speaker, author of *Out of the Saltshaker and
into the World* and creator of the Live/Grow/
Know course and series of books

'These devotional guides are excellent tools.'
John Risbridger, Minister and Team Leader,
Above Bar Church, Southampton

'These bite-sized banquets . . . reveal our
loving Father weaving the loose and messy
ends of our everyday lives into his beautiful,
eternal purposes in Christ.' Derek Burnside,
Principal, Capernwray Bible School

'I would highly recommend this series of
30-day devotional books to anyone seeking
a tool that will help [him or her] to gain a
greater love of scripture, or just simply . . .
to do something out of devotion. Whatever
your motivation, these little books are a must-
read.' Claud Jackson, *Youthwork* Magazine

Available from your local Christian bookshop or **www.ivpbooks.com**

Food for the Journey THEMES

The Food for the Journey: Themes offers daily devotions from well-loved Bible teachers at the Keswick Convention, exploring how particular themes are woven through the Bible and what we can learn from them today. In a convenient, pocket-sized format, these little books are ideal to accompany you wherever you go.

Available in the series

Joy
Elizabeth McQuoid
978 1 78974 163 6

Persevere
Elizabeth McQuoid
978 1 78974 102 5

Pray
Elizabeth McQuoid
978 1 78974 169 8

'A rich feast! . . . We can still have joy in Jesus, even when there are tears in our eyes.'
Edrie Mallard

'I have had the JOY of reading this book in advance and I am excited.'
George Verwer

'Packed full of essential theology, especially important when the going gets tough . . . There's no "junk" here. It's all "food", essential for our walk with God, whatever the terrain.'
Catherine Campbell

'The ideal reboot for a flagging devotional life . . . warm and biblical practical.'
Julian Hardyman

'What a great way to spend a month, studying prayer with such a wide range of applications.'
Karen Soole

Available from your local Christian bookshop or **www.ivpbooks.com**

Related teaching CD and DVD packs

CD PACKS

1 Thessalonians
SWP2203D (5-CD pack)

2 Timothy
SWP2202D (4-CD pack)

Colossians
SWP2318D (4-CD pack)

Ezekiel
SWP2263D (5-CD pack)

Habakkuk
SWP2299D (5-CD pack)

Hebrews
SWP2281D (5-CD pack)

James
SWP2239D (4-CD pack)

John 14 - 17
SWP2238D (5-CD pack)

Numbers
SWP2317D (5-CD pack)

Revelation
SWP2300D (5-CD pack)

Romans 5 - 8
SWP2316D (4-CD pack)

Ruth
SWP2280D (5-CD pack)

Available from www.essentialchristian.com

Related teaching CD and DVD packs

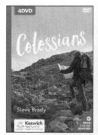

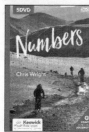

Colossians
SWP2318A (4-DVD pack)

Ezekiel
SWP2263A (5-DVD pack)

Habakkuk
SWP2299A (5-DVD pack)

John 14 - 17
SWP2238A (5-DVD pack)

Numbers
SWP2317A (5-DVD pack)

Revelation
SWP2300A (5-DVD pack)

Ruth
SWP2280A (5-DVD pack)